A Life to be Lived

Lennon Watkins

BookLeaf Publishing

India | USA | UK

Presentation by *BookLeaf Publishing*

Web: www.bookleafpub.com

E-mail: info@bookleafpub.com

ISBN: 9789363312258

First edition 2024

To all those who wants someone to understand
them

ACKNOWLEDGEMENT

I have many people to thank for everything. My family is who I choose to thank first. My parents have always been encouraging, especially when it came to writing. They have never held me back and have put in a great amount of effort to ensure that I am happy and that I have a shot at fulfilling my dreams. My sister is also encouraging but in her own way. She will tell me when I am wrong with no hesitation but, it still encourages me to do better. I also have my friend, Andrea Horner to thank. I wrote my first poem after her passing and that's when I realized I loved writing poems and loved the way a couple of words could affect so many people. I also would like to thank my friends who inspired so many of these pieces.

PREFACE

I write poetry because of the effect it has on other people and for me, it's a quick way to get emotions out. I love how just a few words can make people cry, smile, laugh, or just think about something differently.

The Way of life

How tiny and insignificant our past can feel
Yet how vast and terrifying our future can be
We plan out our lives so quickly
It's as if we are scared that once we decide what
we want, it'll be too late
Like the clock of life ticking down to our final
moment
But the cards dealt to us aren't always
convenient
So when our plans fail,
People turn to the Lord to figure out their lives
When most don't truly trust in what he has
planned
People don't look around to see all the
opportunities that lie just beyond them
They don't look at all the experiences that we are
meant to have
So walk through the valley of life just a little bit
slower than you were before
Stop to see the beauties of the world and enjoy
what we have been given

Love Never Leaves

In a way, love is more than an emotion
It's a feeling, an action, a devotion, a memory
But it can also be a heartbreak
Love is not always mutual
You can feel a love for someone so great
But then get ripped apart when they barely
notice you
You question yourself over and over about the
things that you could have done wrong
And overthink about all the things that you
should have done differently
Their existence is forever engraved in your brain
because... love never leaves
Love is always there reminding you of what
could have been
Love is noticeability
You recall all the little things that you love about
someone
And those little things are like jabs to the heart
Because they will never be yours
Over time, the pain can dull
Until you remember the way you used to look at
them
Love never goes away
I guess that's the risk of loving someone

Once they are there, you cannot get them out of
your head
Their sweet smile, daring eyes, gentle hands that
you once thought to be yours,
forever out of reach
Because in reality, you will love someone for all
the days of your life without them even thinking
about you

The Effects of a Memory

You remember all the big moments
All the activities that we can never forget
But do you remember the small ones
That one conversation, The one science class,
that one recess
I know I do
I don't think I will ever forget
The huge smiles that covered our faces
The tears that poured down our cheeks
Just you alone can never leave me
I will not let it
Without you, I can not be me
So I hold onto them
I hold onto the memories because, without them,
I don't know where I would be
Without them, there is no hope that I would be
able to come back and relive them
Each one means something different
And each one teaches a new lesson
Not all were made out of love
Yet I still hold every single one near and dear to
my heart
Now you can forget me and forget all the things
that we once shared
It will not matter to me
As long as I remember what we used to be

Loving Yourself

I see the others that I admire without a doubt
The ones with perfect teeth, amazing posture, a
likable personality
I used to see them all ranked above me
I, being at the bottom of the list with no perfect
qualities
I could never match up to what they were
But in those times of insecurities, I had to hold
onto the little beams of light
The little things that I had that nobody else did
Over time, Those things became something
bigger
Something that I started to love
Ever so slightly, I began moving up on my list
And then forgot the list entirely
That list was holding me back
People's standards are almost always
unreachable
So I started making my own
My standards, my rules
I realized what I had to get rid of in order to
succeed
Self-judgement
The problem was, I was always wondering what
it would take for them to love me
When I just needed to learn to love myself

There You Are

The beauty of the stars, how bright and as
brilliant as you
The calmness of the waves, always there but
forever moving
Everything there is resembles you in a way I will
never understand
How can a single person reflect so many things
in one's life
You shine in the sun glowing on my skin
The sound of the wind reminds me of your voice
Powerful but beautiful
Without even trying, I see you
I see you in every rainstorm
I see you in the fields of flowers
I see you in the chords of music
We could be miles and miles apart and yet, there
you are
I didn't realize how much of an effect that you
have on me
Until I looked around and glimpses of you were
in everything that I could see

Today

Today will be brighter
We will wake to the sunrise and enjoy all the
colors blended together
The birds will sing, announcing that a new day
has begun
We will forget what we have endured and focus
on what lies ahead

Today will be brighter
We will not waste this opportunity of waking up
We will do the things that we enjoy without a
care in the world
We will message those that we love
And blast music just to dance
Because... why not?

When given ONE life, Why not make it better
At least that is what I hoped for it to be
Today will be brighter
I am determined to do it for me

You

Many people in this world have affected me
greatly
But you... Oh what you have done is
catastrophic
I can not go a single day without you coming
across my mind
I do not know where I would be if you had not
talked to me that day
That day when I was broken and struggling
Oh how times would be different if we had not
crossed paths
I think about it all the time
All the memories we have made
All the laughs we have shared
Even all of our arguments
I am grateful for all of it
One conversation with you can brighten my day
Therefore, I am forever glad that I had the honor
of meeting you

It's Too Late

In the moment, I didn't care
Selfishness overruled my emotions and I didn't
stop to think about how you would take it
How fast it flew by
One day you were the person of my dreams
And the next, I saw you walking away without
turning back
I felt my soul rip in two as the other half of it
strode away
You were gone but still vacated my dreams
Your presence is still with me, but not
I don't know what I can do to fix this
Since I was the one who started the storm
I was the one who practically forced you to
leave
And now I can't help wanting you back
Just one more look at your eyes, those beautiful
field green eyes
And I think I could be ok
I kept denying it
I didn't want to face it
But I can't put it off any longer
Though it breaks my heart
My fragile, selfish heart
I think what you and I used to be...
It's just too late to fix

Still Beating

I have to remind myself a lot that my heart is
still beating
I am not done yet
There is a reason that I woke up this morning
A reason for me to do the things that I do
The world is not over after one little mistake
I know because my heart is still beating
I am still here
This is a grace
We can prosper and learn from our mistakes
We have the opportunity to
Because the thing that pumps blood throughout
our body
The thing that feels too much but shows so
little...
Is still beating
We just can't take it for granted

You Are Rare

I have met many people in my life
Kind ones, soft ones, arrogant, selfish
None of them stuck
Except you
You just kind of showed up one day
Possibly God sent you as a saving grace
All I know is that you are different
You couldn't care less about what others thought
You never hid your laugh or your smile
You had your own way of doing things, your
own style
I admired you for it
You didn't notice, but I and many others did...
You aren't the same as everyone else
You are rare
And I loved it

I'm Stuck in the Past

No matter how hard I try, I can't escape what
used to be
It's like my mind won't let me
Or my body is trying to tell me something
I keep forcing myself to look at what's ahead
But then everything turns back to the past
The people I knew
The experiences I had
The things I should have said
I don't know how to turn away
It's like I'm watching a movie of someone else's
life that I've seen a thousand times
And it's drowning me
All the should've, could've, woulda's
I can't seem to put it behind me
All the things I once had
The dread and guilt I now have
Thinking about it, I want to go back
Go back to the small life when I simply didn't
care
But I can't
I need to learn to move forward
But again, I can't...
I'm stuck in the past with no way out

I Haven't Been Sleeping Lately

I haven't been sleeping lately
Too many thoughts running through my brain
Not allowing me to sink into the darkness and
dream
The days' treasures occupying my mind not
wanting them to be over
But they are...
No amount of dreaming can take me back to
those moments
Yes there will be brighter times, but I don't want
those
I want what was
Now it is just a memory
The only thing I can hope for is these
experiences appearing in my dreams
But in case they won't,
I'll stay up thinking about them,
Which is why I haven't been sleeping lately

No One Understands

I can't help wondering if someone understands
If someone gets how difficult life can sometimes
be
I've been searching and searching for that person
Seeking reassurance that I'm not alone
But I've yet to complete my quest
The longer I go without answers, the closer I get
to breaking
To shutting down
I don't know know if I can take it much more
Feeling such isolation,
So why should I even try
I desire a life worth living,
But I can't help feeling that no one understands
And maybe... No one ever will

There is Hope

No matter how hard life seems, there is still
hope
When you feel like you're surrounded by
darkness,
Just look around you
There will be light somewhere
As tiny as it might be, there is still a spark
Now you can tell yourself over and over that
you're done
That there's no point
That everything you've accomplished was for
nothing,
But you would be wrong
There is a point to life,
There is hope...
You just have to look for it

Your Brightness

When I wake up without even wanting to move,
I just have to think of your smiling face and I
instantly get up
When I'm not motivated to do anything,
I think how proud you would be to have fulfilled
my desires
Just thinking about you puts me in a better mood
Every time I'm with you, it's completely
impossible to be sad
You have such a way of comforting people that I
can't help but want to be with you 24/7
You laugh is contagious
Your faithful and bold eyes
And your soul... extraordinary
I can never say no to you
You could convince me to do anything and I'd
agree
Because you only live once
I might be in the darkest moment in my life
No hope, no desire
But here you are, still shining
I don't know how to say it other than...
Your brightness makes my day better

I am Afraid

I'm afraid of my future
What if I fail and no one sees me the way I want
them too
What if I'm alone and I pass without anyone by
my side
What if I take advantage of life and lose all my
joy

I'm afraid of the past
What if what I did wasn't good enough
What if my past experiences don't prepare me
for success
What if everything I said haunts me for the rest
of my days

I'm afraid of disappointment
What if they look down on me because of one
small, insignificant mistake?
What if my little me doesn't like what I've now
become
What if no one respects me because I didn't do
enough

There are so many "what ifs" in life
The more we focus on them, the more afraid we
are
What if we just let them go
Our life will become more - livable...
Won't it?

Before You

I always wonder about before
Who I was before you
How I acted, what I said
But I can't
Come to think of it, you were always just... there
So I don't know what I was before
Before you showed up and changed my whole
life to what it is now
You have such an influence on me that it makes
me never want to leave you
I don't know what I would do if you up and left
one day
I don't know who I'd be
Because without you, I'm nobody
It's always been me and you
It's never just been... me

I Miss That Day

I think about it a lot,
What happened that day
That wonderful day that's forever engraved in
my mind
I can't stop thinking about it actually
I remember the way you looked at me
The way you made me laugh
The way the smiles never let our faces
I can't remember the last time I was ever that
happy
And I don't think there will be another time like
it
At least, not for a long time
I miss that day
That day between me and you
I miss it a lot

I'm Lonely

I didn't realize until now how lonely I felt
Not alone... but lonely
There is a difference
You can be alone, but not feel lonely
Lonely is a different feeling
A sort of emptiness that no one can fill
I don't know what the cure is
I don't even know if there is one
I just want out
I want to feel understood
I want someone to be my person
But that's not exactly something you find on the
side of the road
You have to search for it
But I don't know if I have the motivation
Or you can just wait for them to come to you
But I don't think I have the patience
I hate to admit it, but I've come to terms with the
fact...
That I'm lonely

I'm Sorry

I don't know how else to say this other than...
I'm sorry
I didn't truly know the effect I had on you until I
saw what I did
How I made you feel
I'm sorry...
For the way I acted
For my arrogance and selfishness
For I didn't think what it would do to anyone but
myself
And now you're gone
You left a void in my life that I thought you had
once filled
So, I'm sorry
For all the things I've done
And for pushing you away
I'm not just saying this in hopes of getting you
back
But in hopes - that you might one day find the
will to forgive me

I'm Proud of You

I'm proud of you
Of who you've become
And who you're meant to be
Of how you act and how you think
Of your drive for success
And your eagerness to learn

I'm proud of you
Even on your lazy days
and when you have no motivation
When you think that you're not worth it and
want to give up

I'm proud of you especially then
Not because you want to quit... but because you
won't
I'm proud of you,
All of you